Twelve Grapes for the New Year

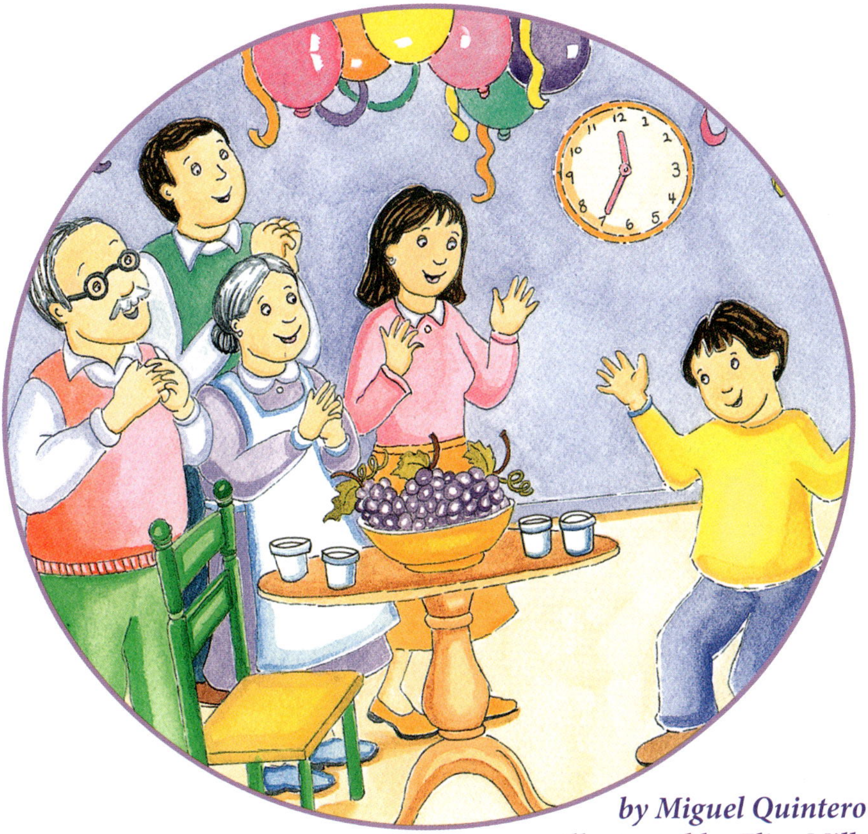

by Miguel Quintero
Illustrated by Elise Mills

PEARSON
Scott Foresman

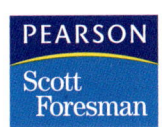

Editorial Offices: Glenview, Illinois • Parsippany, New Jersey • New York, New York
Sales Offices: Needham, Massachusetts • Duluth, Georgia • Glenview, Illinois
Coppell, Texas • Sacramento, California • Mesa, Arizona

　　Benito and his family were ready to celebrate the New Year.
　　"It's almost midnight, Benito," Grandfather said. "Get twelve grapes for you and twelve grapes for me."

Benito went to the table to collect the grapes. He pulled the grapes from the stem. He put twelve grapes into a cup.

Benito pulled twelve more grapes. He put them into another cup. One cup was for Grandfather, and the other cup was for Benito.

"Why do we eat twelve grapes at the New Year, *Abuelo?*" Benito asked.

He called his grandfather *Abuelo*. *Abuelo* is the Spanish word for grandfather.

"Think about it, Benito. How does the number twelve match the New Year?" Grandfather asked.

"There are twelve months in a year," Benito said.

"This is true," said Grandfather. "And how do grapes taste?" he asked.

"Grapes taste sweet," said Benito.

"So why do you think that we eat twelve grapes as the New Year begins?"

"I know!" said Benito. "Each grape is for one month of the New Year. We eat the grapes to wish that each month of the New Year will be sweet!"

"That is a good answer, Benito," said Grandfather. "I have been eating twelve grapes at the New Year since I was a little boy. It is one of my favorite Spanish traditions."

At midnight, everyone cheered. They ate their grapes.

"Happy New Year, *Abuelo!*" Benito said.

"May the New Year be sweet!" said Grandfather.